the 6 figure schedule

*Streamline Your Schedule
and Skyrocket to Six Figures
Using the Science of Iridology*

Debra Angilletta

Published by Imagine Enterprises, LLC
204 E. 22nd St
Cheyenne, WY 82001
(623) 850-4459

www.anewviewllc.com

Printed in the United States of America
First Edition: October 2014

Library of Congress Cataloging-in-Publication Data
Angilletta, Debra
The Six Figure Schedule: Streamline Your Schedule and Skyrocket to Six Figures Using the Science of Iridology

ISBN: 978-0-9960588-7-2

Cover design by Imagine Enterprises, LLC

I LOVED working with Debra on this book! She is brilliant, beautiful (inside and out), and boldly teaching women what they truly need to know about how to operate from their own unique wiring. Debra's style is the perfect combination of smarts and sass. She may be a left-brain Wall Street-savvy business coach, yet she also speaks from the wisdom of the heart. You need this book. You need Debra. You need to learn your way to your 6 Figure Schedule!

Kelly Epperson, New York Times best seller; book coach for Larry Winget & Suzanne Evans "Hell Yeah Star" program; founder birththatbook.com

The Six Figure Schedule is truly an eye-opener! Packed with real world advice, Debra is changing how business people manage their time. Find out what kind of entrepreneur you are and make it work for you. Whether you are a new, or a well-seasoned entrepreneur, this book will teach you how to run your business without sacrificing your family time or social life.

Darrell Knoch, Bestselling author of Mastering a Healthy Self Image and Real Estate Millionaire

The Six Figure Schedule is the entrepreneur's answer to the fears, uncertainties and doubts that keep us stuck. Even if you've been in your own business a long time and have been 'managing', this book takes you beyond managing and into truly succeeding. If you have entertained the idea of needing a new perspective or different way of balancing work and 'life', then this book holds the key to that success. Take a deep breath, honor your deepest desires for your life, and let Debra's down to earth, laser focused, and real life strategies guide you there.

Loren Gelberg-Goff, LCSW, author, speaker, founder
lorengelberggoff.com

To my daughter, Ava:
I knew you were coming, and believed my
life would never be the same. You pushed me
across the Rubicon. I love you.

Contents

Acknowledgements:

To my husband, Peter - who continues to surprise me even when I think the hat has run out of rabbits. Who lets me be me, believes in every decision I make, even if I don't quite believe in them myself.

To my mom, Gail & step-father, Jim - who tolerated my never-ending questions as an inquisitive kid. Always knowing what to say and how to say it, and giving me enough rope to make my own mistakes and find my own way.

To my dad, Guy - who never stopped asking me when I was going to become CEO of the company, and who continues to teach me in the afterlife (I'm listening).

To my grandmother, Jeanette – who has taught me the power of intention, having purpose, and the value of family.

To my brother, Scott & sister, Michelle – my comic relief who lives life without rules and inspires me daily, and who has hearts bigger than Texas.

To all of my friends, family, and colleagues - you tell me the truth when I need to hear it, and then buy me cocktails afterward.

To my extended family - we may not be bound by blood, but we are bound by love.

To all of my teachers and mentors - thank you for creating possibilities for me to walk through.

Introduction

Ah, the corporate life. Steady paycheck, company credit card, and fancy lunches with clients. Life is good!

Then comes the sixty-hour work weeks, sleeping with your Blackberry, countless meetings, and interacting with people you pretend to like so you can be a "team player."

Living the dream?

Not so much.

Waking up to go to work in my mid-thirties, I felt something was missing. But I couldn't quite figure out what was wrong with me.

I was taught from childhood what success looked like and what it was supposed to feel like. I was now living "success" and yet all I could think was *Are you kidding me? Is this it? Is this what I signed up for?*

One weekend, I was at home cleaning out old papers from a box I had leftover from college. I found an old calendar planner. It was from 1993. Everything was scheduled in that planner, and I mean everything. My classes, the jobs I worked, deadlines for papers, and timelines for tests.

It was startling to notice that there wasn't much white area on the calendar. I had literally booked every hour of every day with something. I went to school full time and held down four part time jobs. If I didn't know this was my own calendar, I would have wondered who is this nut job. Apparently my business degree wasn't the only thing I received that year…I was also walking out with a master's degree in the art of cramming ten pounds of sh*t in a five pound bag.

You see, if I wasn't busy, I thought I was lazy.

That's the voice that relentlessly played over and over again in my head on a daily basis. So I just kept moving! That's how to climb to the corporate ladder until you reach success, right? That's what I was taught all my life at home and in school.

If you work "really hard," you'll achieve your goals and finally "make it"! It was a winning formula, and it was tattooed all over my subconscious.

Fast-forward fifteen years, working at my corporate gig on Wall Street. I'd leave the house with my hubby each day at 5:00 AM to commute into New York City from the 'burbs of New Jersey. I'd be at my first client by 7:00 AM with breakfast in tow before the stock market opened. Then back at the office watching trading screens and calling clients to make sales.

Noon rolled around and we were often treated for lunch so we didn't have to leave our desks. When the market closed at 4:00 PM, it was out for cocktails and dinner with clients. The car service usually got me home just shy of 11:00 PM. Just in time for bed so I could do it all over again the next day.

Sounds like fun, right? I was making some healthy ching. No complaints there. But the bank account was just about the only healthy thing going on.

In the middle of all of this busy-ness, my hubby and I came up with the genius idea to have a baby. Why not, right? C'mon… that five-pound bag still had some room!

But here was my reality check. I was thirty-six years old. My adrenals were shriveled up like raisins, my hair was falling out, and the doctors said I would never conceive on my own in my "peri" menopausal state.

But I am super woman…I can do anything!

How wrong I was.

I came by this "working hard" mentality honestly. My father had set the example. Growing up, I saw him travel all the time, and constantly being paged in the middle of the night by big companies needing him to fix hardware failures by the time the sun came up in the morning.

Work was what he did, and the money defined who he was.

I was taught this is how you make a good honest living.

Too bad it boiled down to not so good at all.

My dad worked until he retired. His retirement was not by his choice.

Here's how the plan unfolded - he was diagnosed with diabetes in his late forties, then had two heart attacks in his fifties. His retirement plan was put into play by disability. The choice was made for him. He had dreams like everyone else, with his list of things he would do "someday." Someday never came. My dad died in 2008 at the age of sixty-three.

That very same week, my long-awaited pregnancy that we had put all of our hopes and dreams on, ended. I was in the middle of a miscarriage while trying to tend to my father's final arrangements.

2008 was full of personal tragedies, but it turned out to be the best year of my life.

I discovered that the old belief of working hard for the money wasn't the way to play the game at all.

What if we were to reverse engineer the model?

How about working when you want to, not because you have to? And doing the things you want when you want?

Why live your life doing things you don't want to do? Think about it…does this make any sense?

I was done with making my "someday" list; I was ready to turn them into todays. And opting for a different retirement plan in the process. I was going to make my choices and live now.

That's what made me become an entrepreneur. I ditched the corporate gig for the freedom and the flexibility to play the game my way. And I wanted to do so while still able to make a contribution to the world.

When I say it's reverse engineering, it's true. I had to retrain my brain. Because I still believed the harder you worked, the more successful you were. Because I still believed that if I was not busy, I was lazy.

Does that sound familiar to you?

I was ready for a better way. A little over a year after back to back losses, my husband and I finally had the gift of a little girl. Our daughter was born in 2010 and I wanted to be there with her for everything...the milestones, the breakfast conversations, and even as the mom taxi service that does the drop-offs and the pick-ups at school.

So I had to let go of that old belief of working hard, busting ass, or this wasn't going to work.

I realized it wasn't about trying to squeeze more hours out of the clock, and trading time for money. It was how to use the time I had in a productive way. And not letting excuses, other people, or guilt, rob me of it.

And I've done it. I work from home and plan my schedule around my life - and I actually have a life now! I have lunch with my daughter every day, I make time for my Pilates classes, date nights with the hubs, and time for family and friends.

I've created a six-figure business working four days a week, three weeks a month. I've learned how to make my career work for my life, and me. That's what I help my clients create. That's what I am going to share here with you now.

This book - and this new way of operating - is for you if you're done with your schedule running you. You're the captain of this ship! Honor that desire for flexibility as a business owner. Do what you want to when you want to. It's all in your power; and don't let anyone else tell you any different!

This is a radical mind shift for most. You've probably already realized that being "busy" does not necessarily mean you're productive. (That's what your corporate gig was for!) Yet we still fall in the busy trap.

Now as an entrepreneur, things can be different. You have control over your schedule and your life, yet many entrepreneurs have not figured that out. They still operate with the mentality that you must always be working or you won't be successful. They put more pressure on themselves now than they had in corporate.

Throw that way of thinking out of the window! Know that there is a better way. You don't have to just dream of attracting your ideal clients. You can do it. It starts now. With a strategic schedule, what I call your "Six-Figure Schedule", you will see clients when it works for you, and you will attract the right clients that energize you all day long.

Sound good?

If you are ready to start receiving the money you want and deserve, without killing yourself in the process, you're in the right place. And if you're ready to leave a footprint that impacts future generations, read on. How you create your life not only affects you and your quality of life, you also leave a lasting legacy.

Your last requirement? To have fun! What's the sense of busting your butt and making money if you can't have fun with it?

We left our corporate jobs to be our own boss, not to be a slave to our clients or the calendar. It's time you take back control. Relax and have fun too!

I'm your guide as I have navigated these waters and know what to do, and more importantly, what NOT to do. It can be rough or you can learn to have smoother sailing. Listen, I know I am not for everyone. If I'm not your cup of tea, that's okay. If you want to stay on the treadmill of working hard for "someday," that's your choice. Maybe you just don't believe it's possible, a six-figure schedule on less than sixty hours a week. My goal is to at least create that possibility for you…no matter how far fetched it seems right now.

No matter where you are in your business, if you can take away, at the very least, one great idea that will give you back at least one hour every day, then it's a win/win for both of us.

Even that would be an improvement from where you are now, but it's my hunch that are you ready to take control of your career and your schedule and your life. You are willing to try new things and find what works for you. You are willing to STOP doing things that only keep you in busy mode. It's my goal to help you create your own "Six-Figure Schedule" so you can live life on your terms.

All I'm saying is…enjoy your friends and family now, because when the chips are down and the lights are out…that's who is there in the end. Why not celebrate the good times while you can?

Welcome to your someday…..the time is now.

Chapter 1
Congratulations!

First, let me start out by saying congratulations, you smart little Chiquita! It takes so much courage to even consider stepping into this space of putting yourself out there as an entrepreneur. Many people choose to work for someone else for the rest of their career, and that's okay! On the other side of that, learning how to make money in your own business is an extremely powerful skill set. It will serve you well, and you are in the right place to do that.

So pop on some Kool and the Gang and have your own little "Celebration". Oh yeah!

What you have also chosen is to create something that serves you first. Yes, you come first in the entrepreneurial equation. It's quite a shift from your corporate gig! But a fulfilling one, so start to open yourself up to that.

I'm sure you are filled with the excitement of serving your people. The enthusiasm comes out of every pore of your body, and your excitement is just magnetic.

1

Hold on to that enthusiasm through your first few years in business. It's what keeps you going when the going gets tough. It will be challenging…but only at times. You can implement the strategies I'm about to teach you and you will find you ride the challenges more easily.

Be in it to win it…everything that you want and deserve. The key to getting all of that— and sustaining it — starts with creating ease for yourself from the start.

Your corporate career taught you to work hard. And now in your own business, working hard takes on a new meaning. You can choose to do things the hard way, or the smart way.

Personally, I was done hanging out with the hard way. The hard way just buys you more wrinkles, and who needs that? And if you are reading this book, you're done too. So why not make it easy on yourself?

Be ready to wrap your head around business in a new way. Many of the things I talk about are counterintuitive from everything you learned in your corporate life.

This book is a bit different from the other "how to" books. They usually talk about all the things you need to be doing. I tell you all of the things you need to NOT be doing.

You will soon discover that when you set yourself up from the beginning with the right habits, you won't wind up with bigger problems later. You can stay in love with your business, and also have time to love your life!

So be warned. And be prepared. I'm not here to blow smoke up your behind. And I'm not here to be your best friend that tells you what you want to hear. I am here to tell you the truth around what is possible and what you can have.

Let's dive in!

Remember back to your schooling days? There was a specific curriculum and standards you had to meet in order to "pass" on to the next level. Do you remember where most of your focus was placed? It was mostly in the subjects or areas we did not do well in.

If you were a bad test taker, or didn't get good grades in all of your subjects, it was frowned upon. Remember those mantras that were played over and over again in your head: Bring up those grades! Put more effort into that class (that you hate!).

So I'm here to tell you that in a nutshell, those mantras started our years of self-abuse. The pressure you have continued to put on yourself is not your fault. It actually began all of those years ago. School solidified this perception of focusing on our faults. Because we were on the gold standard back then! "Gold star" standard, that is. If we got the A, we got a gold star. And we've been chasing gold stars ever since.

Does this sound like the easy way of learning to you?

Not me! We can take a new look at how we do things! Here's the first thing I want you to do. Take a deep breath. I am taking out my magic wand and waving it over you. First, throw away all of those lessons you were taught in school.

Second, you are hereby granted permission from this day forward to do the following: Focus on all that you've got, and forget what you are not.

It's time to get clear on what you are good at, and what you really love.

This is how we begin today, right here, right now. Why is that important? Because if you are going to step into being an entrepreneur, it's time to start opening yourself up to doing the things you want to do. There are enough challenges involved in having a successful business, and here is an area you can go easy on yourself from the get go. It makes it a MUCH easier road to navigate.

There are no grades, no gold stars, and no bonus evaluations. No more re-taking a test to bring up that grade. You don't have to keep focusing on the things that are not your strengths. It's time to focus on what you are good at.

I know the next question you may be thinking: "How do I figure out what I'm really good at?"

So glad you asked!

Chapter 2
The Discovery

I discovered something in my thirties that literally changed my life. I'll get to that in a minute. First let me set the stage as to why my discovery was so pivotal for my business, my clients, and me.

I was that kid in school who was smart, but couldn't test her way out of a paper bag. Put multiple-choice questions in front of me and I froze like a Popsicle. My summer calendar was filled with tutors in subjects like science and social studies. A big sigh for a kid in high school who just wanted to work and make some money so I could zoom around in my hot rod with my friends.

My SAT scores were a disgrace. My score was 690. That was my combined score for math and verbal. You would have thought I showed up to write in my name, and then left. But no, I had the prep classes under my belt. I studied and I tried to take that test with the spirit of doing my best.

This "defeat" followed me all the way into my beginning career as a stockbroker. There was licensing involved, which meant it was test time again! And once again, I failed the test, and even lost jobs over it.

However, regardless of how these challenges showed up for me, I always figured out a way to make it work. I took the direction of focusing on what I could do, to create another path for myself.

What I discovered was that I was a visual learner, and not a great reader. As long as I got paired up with teachers who were animated, told stories, used the chalkboard, I noticed I could do better on their tests. Because the way I learned was like creating a movie in my head. When I needed to retrieve information, I'd just play the movie to find the answers. I showed up to class, took notes, and focused on studying the notes, and I could get by!

What kind of learner were you? Have you ever even thought about it?

I also discovered I had a need for collaboration. Meaning, as long as the teacher was there to help me and answer questions in the moment, I was okay. But stick a textbook in front of me, and that was a dead end. That was a one-way conversation with no interaction. I would flounder. High school class success was dependent upon if the teacher taught my learning style.

As you can see from the SAT scores, Harvard wasn't exactly knocking on my door. As a matter of fact, no college accepted me into their four-year establishments. So off to community college I went.

I picked the classes and teachers that fit my visual learning style, yet I realized if I wanted a four-year degree, I'd have to transfer into another school.

I lived at home and decided to investigate options beyond the state schools in my area. My friend attended a liberal arts college locally. Many of her classes involved the same kind of rote learning from high school. Not my cup of tea.

However, they also had a sister school that offered night and weekend classes with adjunct faculty. I could get the same classes I needed to get my business degree yet they would not be the same old "old school" way of operating. Bingo! So even though the business department at the liberal arts school was the size of my thumbnail, I was going!

For the first time, I enjoyed school. I felt like someone finally "got me" and was teaching me the way I could learn. Once I was in my element, I could learn quickly…at lightning speed. It was collaborative and I was learning from professionals in the workforce versus professors teaching from a book.

I loved getting a lot done in a short period of time. I thrived. I could write term papers with ease. The only difficulty was trying to get time on my friend's word processor to print out my papers! This was way before Microsoft Windows and owning a personal computer.   It was either getting time on that word processor or a lot of late nights with a typewriter and correction tape.

School and learning didn't always come easy and it was a long road to discover how I operated. It was a lot of trial and error, and a lot of tears along the way. It's exhausting to even think about it now! But if I had a tool way back then, to help me navigate that road easier, I would have been all over it. And fifteen years after I graduated from college, I actually discovered it!

That discovery actually happened in a learning setting. I am always studying something. While I was still working in my corporate job, I decided to go back to school to study holistic nutrition. The organic thing was hitting the radar pretty hot and heavy, and I wanted to see what this was all about. I thought it would teach me some new recipes to make my new hubby.

Boy, did I get an education! More than I ever imagined. Through that experience, I was introduced to many ancient Eastern methods – around food, healing and scientific studies. Throughout those studies, one modality hit me like a ton of bricks.

I discovered an amazing tool that I now use in my coaching practice today with every single one of my clients. It holds the key to how you operate, how you relate to people, and ultimately your success in business.

It's called iridology.

Chapter 3
Eye-ree-what!?

Pronounce it any way you'd like; iridology is the scientific study of the iris – the color part of your eye.

What lies in there are colors patterns and markings that speak to one's personality and behaviors. It reveals your individual strengths, gifts, but even more importantly, how you operate as a human being and as an entrepreneur!

After the loss of my dad, a colleague decided to get me out of the house, and invited me to coffee. In this coffee shop, they had a community room, like a fish bowl, surrounded by glass. Everyone could see in. I quickly noticed this earthy crunchy looking dude surrounded by gaggles of women giving a talk. What were they so focused on? I snuck in, and heard this guy talking about "iridology". He was speaking from a scientific standpoint. Soon after, I had my own eye mapping done for me, and it literally created a blueprint for my business. It was so powerful for me, I knew I had to study it and share it with others!

Next time you are at the hair salon, open up one of those fashion magazines. Find an up-close picture of a model and look at her eyes. You will quickly be able to see what I mean about patterns and markings in the iris. You may see different colors, freckles in the eye, or even different colored rings.

You have a unique iris, and iridology is the science of reading your eyes. All of those markings can give insight into your personality, as well as how your own internal operating system works. So essentially, it can tell you how special you are.

I won't go into all the details of iridology here, but I can tell a lot from studying the markings of your eyes. From my experience reading hundreds of women's eyes, I've discovered those patterns and markings can identify the type of entrepreneur you are, and I teach how to operate based on your type. Here is where the entrepreneurial types were born.

This would have been useful back in high school, right? What's so wonderful is that iridology can help get you really clear about what YOUR strengths are…so we can have you running on all cylinders with that now!

Knowing your operating system can take you out of the cycle of struggle. No more trying to be something that you are not. No more focusing on what you are not good at. It's time to honor all that you are and use that to its full potential.

It's really exciting and changed my life, and that of my clients. What I've discovered working with countless women business owners is that they fall into one of four major entrepreneurial "types." I call these types Innovator, Caregiver, Heart-Centered and Intuitive.

As we move through the book, I will give the strategies on how you can create YOUR Six-Figure Schedule and you do it according to your type. It's like cracking the code to an easier, more productive life!

Let me give you a brief introduction to each type. Even without looking at your eyes, see if anything resonates with you.

First, we have The INNOVATOR. This person thrives in being a mover and shaker. Picture the cartoon character Speedy Gonzalez – they go a million miles an hour, with precision, and often can't understand why other people don't operate as fast as they do.

They are quick decision makers, and don't need every detail of a story. Their favorite mantra around this would be, "I don't need the labor, just give me the baby." They use time in a way to be most efficient. The more concise, compact and clean you can make something, the better. They love clarity.

One of their major gifts is that they see ahead to the end result faster than the average person. They are true visionaries. These people are the idea generators. Most innovator types use language to say, "I see."

For example, if this is you, know that starting projects is where it stops for you. Put you in a research or implementation situation, you'd rather hang yourself, because now you are already on to the next idea.

You could probably do everything yourself, since you can see how things work in your mind from start to finish. But it doesn't interest you. Just because you can do everything, does not mean you should be doing everything. Know that you do not have to do everything yourself! Creating a team and delegating the working parts of a project is the key to your success.

Also know that you can't take a short cut in surrounding yourself with people who are good helpers. Because you are also money conscious, you might want to go for cheap labor. Don't. You need to hire experts in their respective fields. This will save you time and help you execute your visions in a timely manner. No room for amateur night here.

And don't forget that others do not function like you do. Just because they don't operate at lightning speed, doesn't mean they are not worth your time.

Next, we have the CARETAKER. This is a leader who takes influence from the Beatles – their mantra is "peace and love." They want to be surrounded by people who are always happy, and they have a deep-rooted need to make people happy. If they come upon someone who is not happy, they will stand on their head to make them happy.

They are very generous and will give you the shirt off of their back. They will lend you money before they've even counted it to know if they can feed themselves. They are constant givers. Here is where the Caretaker makes the most difference, but it's a skill that has to be learned to find balance.

They are the ultimate influencers of change by being the change they want to see in the world. Caretakers start out trying to change the world around them by trying to make everyone change "for the better" so that that they will be happy. But they have to learn to be the model for that change, and let people walk their own path. If you are a Caretaker, you can invest yourself in people's journeys, but you cannot invest yourself in their outcome. That is the only way they learn.

Caretakers can see things super clearly. They tend to be able to see ahead for the people around them. Especially those who are on a freight train going two hundred miles an hour heading directly into a brick wall. But their followers have to be ready to hear the message. Their communication style is "I hear you." Since they are such great listeners, they are naturally great storytellers. They are able to connect easily with other through their stories.

Now, for example, if this is you, when you talk to a potential client, think about how you are holding care for them by stepping into their shoes. Only walk around in them for a little bit, and then be sure to take them off and disconnect from their outcome. Helping them will come through your amazing ability to share your own story of how you moved through a major problem and how you got to the other side of it.

The Caretaker is built for service, but you need to remember, you can't always be outputting support. You need to also incorporate getting support as well. Energy is circular. Just like electrical wires, there is an input and an output, and it all has to balance out to light things up.

Caretakers may tend to get in cycles of exhaustion and over commitment, with no time left to nurture themselves. This can also show up in finances, as money will go out much faster than it ever comes in.

The third type is the lovely HEART-CENTERED entrepreneur. They are open and connect easily with people at a deep level and know their most heartfelt desires. No surface conversations for the Heart-Centered. If you have a connection with someone, you can ask him or her questions for hours, just because you are curious, and that's how you connect.

Many of these types were told in their lives to "not ask questions" or "do not pry or be nosey," but the Heart-Centered entrepreneur isn't trying to dig for gossip; it's just the way they connect with people. They have great memories, and will most likely remember your birthday or be able to retrieve information from a prior conversation. They aren't stalking you, it's just the way they file information, and it's just their way of reconnecting and saying, "Hey I remember you and loved getting to know you." They communicate in a way where you will hear them say, "I feel."

Heart-Centered entrepreneurs usually have a devil of a time with sales. It feels unnatural, forced, fake and "why would you want what I have if I just met you two seconds ago." If this sounds like you, throw out the scripted sales pitch, and come to a conversation from a place of helping, not selling. Have your deep conversations. Invite people you want to work with to your office instead of having a conversation by phone. Connecting in person is your speciality, use it!

And other Heart-Centered people will be your best clients, because they will appreciate you connecting at such a deep level. Many times you are considered like family to your clients. Your people will feel that and want to instinctively work with you. Since you are so easy to talk to, you will attract people who will tell you, "I could talk to you for hours," so time management is going to be important for you to learn.

I would not suggest you go into the career of a being professional poker player, because you wear your "heart" on your sleeve. People can easily see on your face how you are feeling. You can also get easily upset by people who are not looking to connect on the same level as you, and you tend to take things personally.

Just remember, not everyone is like you. And also remember that not everything is about you either! So if you come to a conversation where you are trying hard to connect with someone and they just aren't biting, don't beat yourself up like you must have not said the right thing, or thinking you did something wrong. Take yourself out of the equation, because whatever was happening, it wasn't about you!

This will be helpful in your sales conversations when people say no; it's not a rejection of you or your character. It's about them…so leave it with them, and take that off your plate.

Finally, we have the INTUITIVE entrepreneur. This type picks up on details easily, and has a keen sense of everything going on around them. They are like a walking satellite dish, picking up on all the signals around them.

Here's the thing, if this is you, you are able to pick up on all of the good things swarming around, but you can also pick up on people's baggage as well. Be sure to put a practice in place to disconnect yourself from what's happening with other people. Because you have a tendency to take on other people's feeling and thoughts…you are just that powerful!

Your gift is that this sensitivity allows you to see clearly where people are today, and even more importantly, where they can go. Answers come to you so fast and furious; it can get overwhelming at times. Intuitive entrepreneurs, when they aren't clear on their gift, tend to second-guess everything that they think and feel. Why? Because your rational, logical self is telling you that answers can't possibly come this easy for you!

If this is you, just know that you can stop second-guessing yourself. You have the right answers from the start, and it does come that easily to you. The second-guessing will be your biggest expense of energy that can deplete you easily, so it is a skill to hone in and sharpen.

Your communication style will include phrases like, "I sense." Where this amazing gift will show up as a challenge, will be in large crowds of people. Whether at the mall, a wedding, or a convention, things may get overwhelming for you. And if you never knew why, it's because you're like a fine tuned radio tower and you are able to play everyone's station at the same time. Can you see how this can get a little loud and overwhelming?

Here is how you can rein that in a bit - if you have to break away for a moment of silence or peace, do so! Excuse yourself to the powder room and hang out in stall for a spell if you have to. Or excuse yourself for a twenty-minute walk outside. It's okay. Once you start to realize how to manage your gift, it becomes easier.

This is helpful to know if you have to go to networking events. A room full of people milling around probably isn't your ideal setting. So take in a sit-down event, where there are only six to eight people at a table. You only have to connect with the person on either side of you. That can take the overwhelm out of a huge room and break it down to only a few people.

This is just a first-round explanation of the four entrepreneur types. We will be talking more about your type and how to work with it. No more struggle! They say the window to the soul is the eye; the window to how you operate truly can be seen in the eyes! Now you can understand why I was so thrilled to discover iridology!

Which type sounds like you?

Write it down here:

_____

Chapter 4
What's Your Type?

Were you clear on which type you are? Or are you second-guessing your decision? Did you run out of the room to ask a family member, co-worker, or call a friend to validate your choice?

Here's the deal, often when we try to go through exercises on our own, trying to figure out what we are good at, and what makes us special, we start second guessing ourselves. But when someone from the outside sees something in us that we've known all along, we get validation.

It's almost like playing the match game. You have certain thoughts about yourself, and if I objectively pick up on the same thing, it's a match!

It's true and undisputed. It gives that solidifying layer of acknowledgement so we can finally go out and do it! We can be true to who we really are.

Having outside validation is the beginning to getting us moving in the direction we so desire. It's what we sought from our teachers when we were kids... they validated us, they gave us the "gold star." Iridology is so much more. It validates who you are and how you are. Knowing how you operate means you can let go of trying to be something you are not. It validates you to go out and use your strengths. You are wired a certain way and when you function according to that wiring (instead of fighting it!), you can work with more ease, more productivity, more engagement, more reward, more success! And more profit!

Let me tell you a story about a friend I did an iridology reading for. I had known Sarah for almost ten years; we were colleagues back in our corporate life. I knew her apparent strengths in her profession, so it was fascinating what her reading showed. Iridology never ceases to fascinate me.

The discoveries were absolutely amazing. The reading revealed that Sarah was not operating true to her wiring and that is why she was unsatisfied in her corporate career. Her supervisors and colleagues could not see her for who she really is and her strengths were being stifled.

I saw in Sarah's eyes things I never knew about her. She was a creative at heart, and she is someone with strong leadership skills that she's been hiding her whole life. What was interesting is that she actually did know this about herself, but as child, she was taught to hide those skills. As a female, she was told she would never find a man if she was too "bossy." Hence, she kept herself down and why she was where she is today in her career. Sarah had been holding back and not being true to her real nature.

Identifying her strengths and acknowledging where she had been holding back helped carry Sarah to her next great opportunity, (and what she had before her was an amazing one!). Sarah discovered she is a heart-centered type. She loves to connect with people on a deep level. For years, she was involved in a business environment where it was all about face time, with no depth of relationship.

Sarah often wondered why she couldn't connect with people in the course of her job, and she felt frustrated. It's simply the way the business was structured. Her company was playing it the old "safe" way, no one gets beyond face value and no one gets hurt. But for Sarah, she needed to go beyond that and connect with people at a deeper level.

I like to compare her situation to fine furniture shopping. Imagine you have lots of attention from the sales person who shows you around and tells you how the pieces you love are made, all about the materials, the construction, and how it's going to look in a room. That's one kind of experience. That's interacting with people on a deeper level of connection. On the other hand, if you attend a fire sale where the store is trying to liquidate the inventory and things are selling as is, you won't have the same level of interaction.

It's the same kind of scenario with Sarah. She was working for a company that operated at a level of the fire sale, where she needed to be in fine furniture with deeper connections.

But here is what Sarah thought. She thought something was wrong with her and she didn't think she was doing well at her job. There was nothing wrong with Sarah. Her reading made her realize she was not operating true to her internal operating system. She was now ready to step into it. When she put herself out there, and acted the way that was true to her, then everything shifted for her. She ultimately left that company, and found a leadership position where she was valued and her ideas were welcome.

When you start being true to your type, things can begin to break open for you.

Everyone needs this type of validation, especially when you are entering entrepreneurship. You can create anything you want, and it is so much quicker and faster to grow your business when you do it from your entrepreneurial type. If you're not a fan of pain, it's a great way to avoid lots of land mines!

Iridology can cut through self-doubt, save you time, and a heck of a lot of money. I do a reading on every single client. If you are curious and want to learn more, email me at deb@anewviewllc.com and go to 6figureschedule.com/resource

Chapter 5
You Vs. You

Whether you realize it or not, it is truly crucial to begin to understand your entrepreneurial type when starting your own business.

The reality is, when we start in our business, we are still trying to sharpen those skill sets we were never gifted with in the first place. You think you have to do it all and you assume you have to do it a certain way. This starts to set off another cycle, a cycle of comparison.

You begin to question yourself and you start to compare: "I see Jane being successful and I can't seem to get the hang of this!" Now all of a sudden in your mind, it's all going south.

Teddy Roosevelt had something to say about this: "Comparisons are the thief of joy."

Teddy was right. When you compare yourself to others, you're setting yourself up. You're only seeing the surface of someone else's outcome. You have not traveled their journey. So don't bother trying to hold yourself up to some made-up standard your ego is conjuring up for you.

Focus on judging yourself by your ethics, values and gifts, and leave comparisons at the door.

You see? You can do things the easy way or the hard way. And that includes your current state of perception.

There are a ton of great strategies out there for you to use in your business. Many new entrepreneurs try them all, see what sticks and what doesn't. This can be exhausting and expensive. But instead, if you take the time to discover your entrepreneur type, and all of those strengths you were inherently downloaded with, things get easier.

There is always more than one path to get you where you want to go. Walk the path that works for you. You don't have to subscribe to all of the coaching gurus' advice verbatim - "I must do everything exactly like that or else I won't make it." That only serves to get you all tensed up. This will also keep you in the comparison game forever.

You can break free. You can find entrepreneurial success and do it your way, focusing on your strengths.

I've given you a rundown of the four types and the opportunity to discover what you are. Armed with that knowledge, we can explore how to create your business strategies that work specifically for you. Fewer struggles, more successes.

Let's dive into some foundational pieces of creating this Six-Figure Schedule. Keep in mind, it's more about what you need NOT be doing!

This is the number one mistake I see entrepreneurs go off track with early on. It's the big B word...

Boundaries.

When you start getting new clients for the first time, most new business owners want to be flexible, accommodating, and easy to work with so the clients will just fall in love with you.

You take anyone at any time. You work according to THEIR schedule.

But here's the real deal…

If you start plugging in clients when and where they want to see you, and you make concessions and start canceling other personal obligations to take a client, you will start to resent your clients and your business.

I see this all of the time.

I can spot the business owners with a chaotic schedule…they are harried, wishing things were different and saying how busy they are with no time for them.

Just remember, a chaotic schedule attracts chaotic clients.

It's a common mistake. You think you have to bend over backwards to please your client and accommodate their schedule. The thing you need to do FIRST is please you.

Boundaries. YOUR boundaries. Establish them from the get-go. (See what I mean when I warned you much of what I teach is counterintuitive!) Trust that you will still be able to get clients and serve them on your time schedule.

If not, you are setting yourself up for burn out, stress, and resentment.

If you are only set up to be outputting energy constantly to your clients, you are not opening yourself up to re-energize yourself, and you will be on a one-way collision course with burn out. Because energy does not flow one-way. If you don't consciously start by placing those things in your calendar that are going to energize you, then all you are going to do is chronically deplete yourself.

That serves no one.

Here is what happens:
You can't serve at your highest level.
Clients will start to feel unimportant.
Your family will start calling you "Skip."
Time off will come in the form of sick days.

When you are not working at your best, or if you're not working at all, clients will start to fall off, and you can't generate the income you want.

This pattern of "no boundaries" is what you want to start reprogramming. Because your corporate career taught you just the opposite.

Wasn't part of your reason for becoming an entrepreneur the ability to enjoy your life more and have flexibility to do the things you want to do, when you want to do it?

Setting up your personal boundaries is the first critical part of having a Six-Figure Schedule. So here is what you do…before you put any clients into your calendar, put all of your non-negotiables in your schedule.

What are your non-negotiables? What is it that you need to do stay sane, stay happy, stay motivated, and stay glad that you left the corporate world for your own gig? Write them all in your schedule. Your morning workouts, lunch, cocktails with friends, phone calls to mom, trips to the museum with friends, date night with your partner, library day with the kids.

Put it all in your calendar.

Treat each of these like a client appointment. You wouldn't trade one client for another on your schedule would you? So don't do it to yourself – you ARE your best client.

If you do this from the beginning…(or start now) here are a few things I can promise you:

Great clients
Predictable income
Energetic client meetings
Time to get every thing done
Never be resentful of your clients or your business
Enjoy and appreciate all of the opportunities you have before you
Ease around family feeling secure about having exclusive time with them

Now I know you are saying: "But Debra! If I do that, how can I be successful?!"

Start by shutting down that inner voice telling you it's not possible. Because it is.

I've done it and you can do it too. (Did you see my SAT scores? I'm not a rocket scientist.) The most successful entrepreneurs will tell you this too. It's their secret, and that's what they are not telling you!

Just try it! Even if it's hard, put everything you've always wanted to do on your wish list. If money or time were not a factor, fill in that calendar to do the things you want to do. If I gave you a magic wand – what would your ideal schedule look like?

Be creative. List YOUR non-negotiables here:
1.
2.
3.
4.
5.

For example, mine are:

Pilates twice a week
Mondays or Fridays off
End every day by 5:00 pm
No client appointments Saturdays or Sundays
Standing sitter every Wednesday night for a girls night out
Friday or Saturday night date night with hubby
One week a month off from client appointments

I maintain my boundaries so I can be at my best for my clients and my family. Everyone out there is telling you to work hard. I'm telling you to work smart so you can enjoy the fruits of your labor. I promise, you will thank me for it!

Start on your own calendar right now or download the calendar worksheet provided for you at 6figureschedule.com/schedule.

On the top of your calendar, write down the entrepreneur type you are, Innovator, Caretaker, Heart-Centered, or Intuitive. Now, fill in the days and times of your non-negotiables.

This is where it all begins!

Chapter 6
Check Please!

Once you have gotten clarity around your entrepreneurial type and your boundaries, let's start creating what you want to see for an income this year!

We then will work backwards from that figure showing you how to create this for yourself.

Let me use my client Sally as a case study to illustrate this example. Sally is a personal trainer who just decided to hang out her own shingle and opened her own business. One of the first things she stated to me was that she want wants to make $175,000.00 And she said she had figured out how to get there. I like a girl with spunk!

It was a dream of hers, to have her own business, and still make the pay she left at her corporate job. Okay, $175,000.00 Let's see Sally's plan.

Here's what I asked her and her responses:

Q: How many days of the week will you see clients?

A: 7 – I can see people everyday

Q: How many clients can you see in a day?
A: 6

Q: How much are you charging each client?
A: $85.00 per session

Q: What business hours will you keep?
A: Start at 10:00 AM and finish by 7:00 PM

Q: Are you planning any trips or vacations this year?
A: Yes, a two-week training retreat I attend every year

OK…so now let's overlay some simple math to this study.

7 days working x 6 clients each day = 42 clients per week

42 clients x $85.00 per slot = $3,570.00 per week

$3,570.00 per week x 50 weeks in the year (she's taking off two weeks)= $178,000.00

Not too shabby! You're probably thinking that's a nice chunk of change. And yes it is!

So $178,000.00 is Sally's perceived annual income potential.

Let's bring this case study into the world of reality of Sally's plans.

Here are the additional questions I asked her:

Q: Are you driving to see your clients or are they coming to you?

A: I drive to them

Q: What is the average drive time to each client?
A: 30 minutes

Q: How do you get new clients?
A: Referrals

Q: Do you have to do your own workouts to stay in shape?
A: Of course!

Q: Do you have friends and family that you like to see?
A: Yes, I love entertaining

Q: Do you have any dependents?
A: Yes! My beloved poodle named Trixie

Q: Do your clients take vacations?
A: Yes, my clients travel often, 4 or 5 times per year

Now, dear reader, I don't know your SAT scores, but I know you are pretty smart. Can you see where we are headed here?

Based on Sally's answers, here is the reality of what will happen:

Sally in reality can only see 4 clients per day based on her schedule and drive time. Remember, each client one way is 30 minutes. So she has to tack on 1 hour to each client session. So now, each client's session is really 2 hours of her time.

Her clients take vacations too, so that means no business from them while they are gone.

Next, she didn't mention any time for marketing. She is relying on referrals, which are a hit or miss pipeline for her. If she's not marketing herself, she can't keep filling her pipeline to have 4 consistent people all 7 days per week.

Her clients get sick, and she gets sick sometimes too. And having a dog, there are times she would need a day off to take Trixie to the vet.

Opening yourself up to working 7 days per week doesn't take into account the things you have to do for yourself. Your own workouts, getting your laundry done, visiting friends and family – and time to enjoy your life!

So you can see, begin to plan your business life out realistically. It's not about opening your doors and telling people to come any time all the time.

Here's your check – your reality check.

You have to create an energetic balance in your schedule for your three important areas: client service, marketing, and personal life.

I see this simple scenario over and over and over again. It's totally fixable, but just coming to terms of the reality tends to be a bit challenging.

Based on how Sally has her schedule set up now, it isn't in reality going to get her to $178,000.00 this year. She can do it though, and after you learn the strategic tips in this book, you will understand exactly what you need to be doing to hit your numbers year after year with ease.

So let's get this party started…what is your income number you want to make this year?

Write it down here:

_____

There is something about putting good old-fashioned pen to paper and writing things down. Your intentions become clear of what you want to see happen. The act of writing is almost like making an imprint in the universe so that it can get crackin' on your behalf. Looove it!

So, what was your number?

You can see from our case study how most people don't set themselves up for success from the beginning.

Here is where we start crafting a plan to back into these simple numbers, and it will paint the picture of what you need to start doing. Your business will start to tell you a story. It will let you know when things are working and when they are not.

So what do you need as far as a roadmap?

You need to invest in one simple thing. I like to call it your energetic schedule plan.

I hate that old word "business plan." It sounds old and stodgy, and even smells a little musty. And it's just downright exhausting thinking about putting together one of those behemoths. Not fun, and I'm a business strategist!

Let's begin to move through the key areas where you are going to save yourself a TON of time. You can begin crafting your energetic schedule so you can realistically create that Six-Figure Schedule!

Chapter 7
Strangers With Candy

Well, let's start with some bad news. I know you have studied like a good girl scout to become a professional in your area of expertise. All of those trainings and certifications...yep... check, check and check. But there is something no one taught you - especially if you went to MBA school!

Your expertise is only part of the entrepreneurial equation. The rest is...(drum roll please)...marketing and mindset. Whoa! What does that mean?

You can be the best in your area of expertise, but if you can't sell your services, you are going to continue to struggle.

What do you think of when you hear the word "marketing"? When people first started to tell me about marketing, a funny image popped up into my head. All I could think of was riding around in my mom's grocery cart at the store when I was a kid. That's what I knew about "marketing"! That's how foreign this concept was to me.

And the next thing I heard was the all-dreaded activity that I tried to stay away from like the plague. No...don't say it...not that "N" word! Networking!

I began to notice other new business owners had the same visceral reaction as me. Why was networking a scary concept for so many people? My mind just couldn't stop trying to process the answer!

Many business owners share the same questions about this topic. Things like, "What do I say? How do I get people to have conversations with me? How do I keep the conversation going?"

The fear of networking is now something I teach and speak on, and one key nugget is not only surprising, it's downright jaw dropping.

Just know, if you hate going to networking events, it's not your fault!

Here's the deal...you were set up to fail when it comes to networking.

Bombshell.

Making connections is such a critical part of building relationships to grow your business. When we find ourselves caught up in the struggle of talking to people we don't know, we get down on ourselves. Then we start the cycle of blame. Then the inside voice starts nagging you saying, "What is wrong with ME?"

Stop blaming yourself. There is nothing wrong with you. Peter Drucker, legendary management consultant and author said, "More business decisions occur over lunch and dinner than at any other time, yet no MBA courses are given on the subject."

How about them apples.

You were never taught in school how to network. Never.

Oh....and there's more.

Something happened long, long ago that you are not even aware of. Something that lies deep in your subconscious programming that holds you back from being a successful networker.

Do you remember the cautionary statement your parents told you as a kid?

"Don't talk to strangers."

Yep, that's the one!

OK...now what is networking?

It's talking to a room full of strangers!

See a pattern here?

Told ya it wasn't your fault!

So here is what never happened...that file - that message you heard over and over, DON'T TALK TO STRANGERS - was saved to your subconscious database. It was never updated as you got older. It's still running your operating system.

What do you have to do now? Let's rewrite that program!

First, cut yourself some slack. Know that you are not alone in dreading networking, know this skill is something you were never taught, and know that you were in fact taught the opposite of what you now need to do to grow your business.

You can begin to implement some strategies to start connecting with "strangers." These folks are not going to give you candy, but are your ideal colleagues and clients who will give you business.

Again, you operate best when you honor your entrepreneurial type, and this of course applies to networking:

INTUITIVES – Big networking events where there is a sea of people can be challenging for you. Too much energy flying around, and it can cause overwhelm and exhaustion.
Try a "sit down" networking event. These for example, are luncheons or dinners. It can help take the "noise" out of the room that you are so sensitive to. This narrows your focus and those fine-tuned antennas to just connect with the people at your table.

First, focus on connecting with the person on either side of you. After that, aim to connect with the rest of the people at the table. This way you will have walked out with meeting between two and eight new people.

HEART CENTERED – Business events or workshops are great for you because you love connection in person. What tends to leave you feeling unfulfilled is not being able to make a deeper connection with people.

With an all-day workshop, there is a lunch break. This gives you the opportunity to invite someone (or two!) to lunch so you can chat with him or her at length. It's the perfect forum to ask all of your burning questions about the other person to deepen that connection.

CARETAKERS – These people love a good party. Any networking group that is putting on a celebration or a party is your kind of place. Happy, happy, happy, those are the people you like to be around.

Holiday celebrations, cocktail parties, dinner parties, or even a friend's home party (think Tupperware, jewelry)...these are your kind of places. People gravitate naturally to happy people, so be sure to bring along your infectious smile and quick wit.

INNOVATORS – Have you ever heard of "speed" networking? This is right up your alley. Quite frankly, you don't have much patience for networking events. You'd rather be the on stage connecting with many than one by one! But use networking events to connect with the organizer of the group, or seek out other organizers of other groups so you can get on their speaking roster.

Quick note – have you noticed that the INNOVATORS paragraphs are much shorter than the rest? It's because your attention demands that I get to the point! I understand you, my friend, and I'm keeping it short and sweet to honor your entrepreneurial type!

Chapter 8
Magic Numbers

Now that you can get out there and network, you can start to think about the effect of your efforts. You are out there connecting with people for a reason!

Here's the next part of the marketing equation. It's all about the numbers, baby!

You need to have a good idea of how many people you need to get in front of on a monthly basis. To start filling up your pipeline, you have to talk to people or be in front of many people in order to set up a slew of sales conversations.

So how many people do you need to be meeting?

Yep, knowing your numbers starts here.

You can convert your numbers into weekly, or even daily, but I am going to demonstrate monthly in this example.

When you understand the numbers around this, you will see what kind of effort you need to put forth in your business. It helps to have goals, right? Knowing our goal numbers and then getting clear on what we need to do to meet our goals is the winning formula here.

And away we go! Let's use a case study.

My client, Marley, wanted to bring on 5 new clients each month. Totally doable! Let's back into the numbers of how this works so you see what Marley did to get those clients.

It doesn't matter what your goal is, I'm going to give you the magic number - the number **3**. Remember this number, and you can calculate your numbers in any situation.

On average, 1 out of every 3 people that hear you speak or see you teach will result in a sales conversation to talk about your services. 1 out of 3 will be willing to have that conversation with you.

Next, 1 out of 3 of those sales conversations will turn into 1 new client.

These numbers may be wider when you first start, like 1 out of 5 or even one out of 7. That's normal and that's how you know you're getting good…when you start closing 1 out of 3 people you talk to.

Marley first needed to figure out how many sales conversations she needs to get 5 new clients this month. Here's what we did:

5 (number of new clients desired) x 3 (magic number) = 15 (Marley's sales conversations needed)

Next, Marley needed to figure out how to get in front of enough people to get 15 sales conversations. Let's look at the math:

15 sales conversations x 3 (magic number) = 45

Marley needed to get in front of at least 45 people per month where she asks them to have a complimentary consultation with her. To get 5 new clients, it takes 45 people to talk to.

Do you see how her numbers work?

Marley connects with 45 people.
1 in 3 people will agree to have a sales conversation - that's 15 sales conversations. 1 in 3 of those sales conversations will come on as a new client. That's 5, her goal number.

Getting sales conversations is no longer a mystery. Use the magic number 3 and you can run your own numbers.

So now you will ask…how do you get in front of 45 people a month?

Well, I happen to have a handy dandy list. These are all face-to-face marketing strategies. Online marketing strategies are also great and I coach on those too, but building relationships online takes much longer than in person. So for now, let's talk about face-to-face ways to get in front of those 45 people.

The trust factor soars when you put yourself in the position as an expert that can connect with many people at one time. Check out my resource page for some easy ways to get in front of many people at one time: 6figureschedule.com/resource

So let's look at what you want to achieve:

How many clients do you want each month?____

How many sales conversation do you need?____

How many people do you need to get in front of this month to get these sales conversations?____

Now that you know about the magic number 3, you know how to run the formula for your situation. Maybe you want to take on 1 new client a month or maybe you want 10. Do the math to determine how many people you need to be in front of and then pick the strategies to get you there.

Remember you use your entrepreneurial type to refine how you implement the strategy.

Chapter 9

Rent With Option to Buy

Now that you know you have to get in front of a good amount of people each month to generate new clients, which marketing strategies are going to be best for you?

You will do a combination of various options, webinars, speaking, etc. I also am fired up to tell you I've found that there is one universal strategy for all entrepreneurial types. You will make some slight tweaks based on what works for you, but overall you can do very well with this networking/ marketing strategy.

It's **sponsorships**.

You pay to "rent space" as a sponsor at someone else's event. You choose the events that are right for you - the people at that event are your ideal clients. You have a booth or a table where you meet, greet, and have your products or services available for them to buy if they choose.

Sponsorships give you the chance to be in front of many people in one fell swoop. Sponsor opportunities come in many shapes and sizes (and investment levels). Some include a speaking spot but you don't have to get on a stage if you don't want to (but I highly recommend it!). Those of you who aren't fans of doing a public speaking event can be a sponsor and still reach many people.

Let's look at how you can handle a sponsorship based on your type.

Just having a table or a booth is an overall great strategy for the HEART CENTERED entrepreneur. This gives you the opportunity to connect with people in person. Shaking hands, giving a hug, sharing your expertise, it's all about connections and there are lots of them at these events. In-person connection feeds your soul; it's a perfect match.

Some sponsorships can also be a speaking sponsorship. You have a booth and you also have a speaking slot on the stage to address a crowd. You have a set amount of time where you have the spotlight to share your expertise. This is appealing to the INNOVATOR type, since they like to be the center of attention.

Sponsorships come in all sizes. For the INTUITIVE entrepreneur, a smaller event (100 people or less) is a great size crowd for you. Too many people in a room can overwhelm you with all of the activity you may be picking up on. With less people in the room, you can focus better on those people who approach your booth without feeling too overwhelmed. Your gift of inspiring people can reach far with a smaller crowd… it penetrates much deeper on this level. When choosing which events to sponsor, keep the number of attendees in mind. For you, bigger does not always mean better.

The CARETAKER entrepreneur can take a sponsorship with a breakout session. This is where you have a booth, and have an opportunity to highlight your expertise in a smaller room where people will sign up to see you speak. This is the perfect place to tell your stories of your own struggles, and then give people exercises to help move them forward. Assign paired shares so that they can experience your strategies so they can see where they can go.

I love doing sponsorships and I love teaching my clients how to maximize the opportunity based on their type. I of course teach other strategies too. This is just to get you excited to see you are not forced into just one way of marketing your business.

Do you see how there are many ways to get in front of the people you need in order to get the sales conversations, which turn into clients? Can you see that for each strategy, you approach it based on your entrepreneurial type? I love it!

I don't just coach my clients to run out and be a sponsor; I help them see how they can best maximize their energy at a sponsorship to be true to their brilliance. It works that way with all the strategies. You tweak them according to how you operate.

Chapter 10
Market & Sell According to YOUR Type

Once you identify the strategies you resonate with, now you have to create consistency with these strategies. This turns into your marketing calendar.

Start keeping track each month which marketing activities you are undertaking. Be sure you are doing something every month to keep your pipeline moving!

Here's why you do this: There is a wide gap between perception vs. reality. Sometimes we feel like we are not doing enough, so we start getting into overdrive out of fear...and start committing to a lot of events.

My client, Tracey, is really good at creating activity. She's very social, loves to be out and about. She runs workshops, networks three to four times a week, and recently had 2 sponsorships over the last month.

Tracey came to me upset. With all of this activity, she wasn't making money.

We visually mapped out where she was over the past month, and where she had committed herself in the following month. We started to create her marketing calendar.

What we discovered is that Tracey was double booking networking events on the same night, and she committed to two sponsorships that ran back to back. She had a huge list of people to follow up with, but guess what happened? She had so much networking activity that there was no time left for her to follow up and have her sales conversations.

She was on to the next event, and then the next event. Tracey had not scheduled any time to follow up with all her new connections. No more mystery why the money wasn't coming in!

If you don't keep track, you start overlapping commitments, run ragged and get exhausted.

On the other end of the spectrum, you need to maintain a consistent pace. If you participate in a huge event, then become so exhausted from it, you may forget to schedule your next one. Now all of a sudden, your pipeline has dried up!

This strategy of creating a marketing calendar keeps you out of the cycle of feast or famine, and creates consistency in your marketing efforts…no matter what entrepreneurial type!

For the HEART-CENTERED person – be sure you don't over give. You want to be mindful of the clock. Setting a timer during the day will help keep you on track.

The INTUITIVE will need to create breaks and space out your commitments. If you schedule a talk, block out the day before or the day after to rest and rejuvenate.

CARETAKERS can get caught up in doing favors for other people and lose focus on what they need to be doing to drive their business. Commitment to weekly revenue generating activities needs to go into your calendar.

The INNOVATOR just likes to go for it, but you can't bypass the sales conversations! Block out designated times for them and honor that time with potential clients.

I'm excited to give you the insights that I never got when trying to understand what comes out of the other end of marketing - the selling game.

Now that you've met a ton of people and generated lots of buzz, here is where the almighty sales conversations enter the room. Some people call them strategy sessions. The term is not what matters; the purpose is what counts. These brief chats are your opportunity to go deeper to see if you are a match to working with this potential client.

Your entrepreneurial type plays a big role in these conversations. So why not approach it the way you naturally operate? Sales seem like an uncomfortable way of being for many people. And the reason is because there has been a standard "one size fits all" way of teaching sales all of these years! In my book, there is more than one way to skin a cat.

You see, I've never been the salesy type. It was like an itchy sweater I had to put on. I'd rather run my nails down a chalkboard than sell. Selling ran a close race on the pain scale next to networking for me.

Thankfully, I learned it doesn't have to be that way, for me or for you! That's exciting news. Let's go back to our mantra: Work with what you've got...forget what you are not!

Brilliant!

When it comes to selling, you may be thinking, can't I just have someone else do that for me? Not really. It's part of the "getting you know you process." Think about it from that perspective, it can take some of the angst out of your resistance.

The sales conversation is part of creating that rapport with your people. And don't forget, at the core, people do need your services. But, they make their final decision on the "like" factor. They like you! That's why they choose you. So if someone is doing the selling for you, they can't get the full experience of you. It makes it harder for the prospect to say "yes."

Knowing this is a necessary part of the process. The sales conversation is the #1 place most entrepreneurs struggle.

Let's go ahead and look at each entrepreneurial type and give you great strategies around selling that fits how you operate:

INTUITIVE – Engage your prospect in meaningful conversation and be sure to ask a lot of questions. You can do this over the phone or in person.

Ask your potential client to paint a picture of how they want to see their life at the other end of their challenge. Put an imaginary magic wand in their hand and tell them to waive it, and make a wish! Then talk about how you can see what's on the other side of their challenge clearly.

Next, guide your people by showing them how you can get them there by breaking down the path in a step-by-step fashion.

It's the good old example of how to eat an elephant…one bite at a time!

Your people are most likely information processors, and they will have a lot of questions before they make a decision to say yes. Hold that vision of the future for them, and keep bringing them back there.

Here is where you need to be careful. You have the gift of being able to see the solution to other people's problems easily…but you can't solve it for them! And they have to be ready to see it for themselves. If they can't let themselves imagine where they can go, they just aren't ready.

Your clients have to do the work to get the value of out it. Don't be tempted to do it for them! It's important they do the work, and take the actions. Don't get roped into doing work for them, they will ask you! Let them discover it on their own, or else you will take away the lesson from them. Stay in the role as the guide and keep bringing them back to their goals of what they want to see happen. Be the guide on the side.

HEART CENTERED – You feel like a fake, phony, and forced if told to use a sales script. Throw it away! Ask probing questions, deep questions that speak to your prospect's heart. Your ideal clients are other heart-centered people who you may hear say, "I could talk to you forever."

I give my all of my private clients a menu of questions they can ask during the conversation.

Come from a place of helping, not selling, and preferably in person. Speak to their problems from a heartfelt place of how you can help them get to the other side. Use feeling words to communicate this. Ask them how they are going to feel if they don't fix their problem.

Invite them to your office, or meet the really good prospects out for coffee. Do not meet them at their house or place of business. Since you're all about connecting on a deeper level, these environments are ripe for distractions. It won't serve either one of you. Your prospects also love hugs; so if you pick up on that, feel free to skip the handshake. They will welcome it!

Just be careful not to over-give. Pick one problem, solve it, and then use the rest of the problems as an example of how you can continue your work together. Your tendency is to give too much, and if you do that, then they have no reason left to work with you.

CARETAKER – Since you influence people by modeling change, be sure to tell lots of stories. Share your struggles, and the path you took to get to the other side. Stories are going to be your selling strategy, and be sure to use that wicked sense of humor.

Reference another client that had the same problem or struggle as the person you are addressing. Use details from start to finish to help them resonate with the person you helped. Don't skip the details; your potential clients want to hear every nugget. You will have them hanging on every word.

Word things in a way that communicates, "If I can do it…you can do it, and here's how we can do it together."

Then continue to share your own stories and reference that you teach what you have experienced yourself.

Many caretakers are academics, so just be careful to not come from a place of teaching from a textbook, citing chapter and verse. Be sure to work on how you word things to your clients. Don't speak about concepts that are too much over their heads, think about using language a ten-year-old would understand. It's not insulting, your people are only interested in how you can solve their problem, not the science or big words behind it.

INNOVATOR – You can see to the other side quicker than most people. You are able to come up with some really creative ideas! Your ideal people will appreciate your out of the box thinking.

Your ideal clients have an edge or a rebel way about them. They are rule breakers, and speak from this perspective. Blow the lid off of conventional thinking with your ideas…they will love and appreciate your difference.

Your strength is selling in numbers. Selling from a stage is something you can pull off beautifully. Be sure to take a lot of time on your offer at the end of a talk. Don't skim over it; take your time here. Be mindful, your inclination will be to speed through it. Practice, practice, practice. Start by offering complimentary initial consultations, then move up to selling a product or services where people buy on site. Video will also be a powerful medium for you to sell from as well.

Great! So now you have discovered some strategies of how to sell based on how you naturally operate as a business owner. Begin to work from your own natural way of being and you will see your conversations - and your conversions - improve!

Chapter 11
Entrepreneurial Epidemic

Here is a powerful concept for all entrepreneurial types. And this seems to happen to everyone at some point…no one is left unscathed.

You can blame it on your ego. The ego tries to protect us from pain. And where pain can hit us deep at our core is when people won't commit or when they say no to working with us.

Can you feel the air getting sucked out of the room? <Yikes>… <gasp>…<big sigh>.

Entrepreneurs are being affected by an epidemic. At some point in time, we all catch it.

It's called "story-itis."

We take it personally when someone says no. "Did I say something wrong? Did I do something wrong?" The internal voice goes into hyper-overdrive.

You have to take yourself out of the equation. You can't make it about you. Because once you start, you're off to the races. And soon you start to make up a story. A really big, long, drama filled story. Take yourself out of the story. What you are really doing here is making the "no" all about you, when that's not what it's about at all.

I had a client who frequently suffered from "story-itis,. We needed to find a way for Lori to get out of her chronic story. She was on the verge of tears every time I spoke to her. So I took her back to where this started for her. And she's not alone, it happened to you too. Here's the root cause of this epidemic....

Do you remembered the days of dating? Awesome night out.... great meal, great conversation, and you can't wait to see this person again!

But what happens next? Crickets.

He didn't call.

Remember what you did next? You started coming up with seven different ways 'til Sunday of why he didn't call.

"Maybe he's busy at work...."
"Maybe he can't find my phone number..."
"Oh wait, did he say he was traveling this week?"
"Oh no, he could have been hit by a bus and I'll never know!"

We have this tendency to step into the other person's shoes and start walking around in them and coming up with different scenarios FOR THEM.

Our imaginations start to run wild...we make it bigger, and way more involved than it needs to be.

And funny enough, just when you thought those days were behind you....

This is what's showing up all over again in your sales conversations.

Your resistance to the sales process is common. Why? Deep down we are afraid of what will happen.

It goes back to our prior dating experiences – when "they" didn't call.

Failing to be acknowledged that we exist, our subconscious wants to protect itself from that pain.

So what happens next?

Story time!

We still feel the sting of what we think is rejection, so we start with the stories.

"Well, maybe I shouldn't call Great Prospect 'A,' she's probably busy at work; she just bought a new car and probably doesn't have the money to work with me; she's probably working with someone else already…" and every other possible scenario in between.

Take yourself out of the cycle of story time, stop coming up with reasons FOR them. Give your prospects a chance to tell YOU what's going on with them.

If they say YES….celebrate! If they say NO, here's the rest of the story (so you don't have to make one up!): Today's NO can turn into tomorrow's YES.

Be sure to stay in touch with them through a follow up strategy. Put them on your mailing list, and schedule times once or twice a month to reach out personally through an email or phone call. Many times a NO means not right now.

If you are struggling with your sales conversion number... look no further. Here is where you can shift it completely. Come to the call with no focus on you. Be an open vessel for whatever comes out of people's mouths. Coat yourself visually in Teflon, so everything rolls right off of you. Because if you start getting caught up or making up stories that people's stuff is about you...you're cooked. Game over.

The "no" is about them and where they are at right now. And your job is to get them to "Yes" or "No.". Then on to the next. No more story time. This can be the single most important factor and game changer in your conversations.

Chapter 12
Psst…the Money is Here

I want you to reconnect with your WHY again. Why you left your corporate job to have your own business. You ditched your corporate gig to leave behind the sixty-plus hours per week…you didn't trade it in to work in your own business sixty-plus hours a week.

Now that you have people who want to talk to you (sales conversations) and work with you (client appointments) and you have created your marketing funnel to keep the momentum going (marketing calendar), how do you make sure you have the time to do everything you need, and want to do?

The answer? A strategic schedule.

Goodbye to the days of putting people in the calendar "when it works for THEM."

That is the first sign of chaos. You must run your calendar like the CEO you are. Run it carefully, and strategically, because your time is extremely valuable. Why? Because money doesn't land in chaos. It needs a stable home.

A chaotic schedule attracts chaotic clients…who in turn, don't pay. So think long and hard about whom you want signing up to work with you! You don't want just any client - you want your ideal clients! That's what this is all about - attracting the right people to work with you so you create the business you love on your terms.

Remember in the beginning when I told you some of what I teach seems counterintuitive? This is one of those times!

You may be thinking…if you limit your time and structure a schedule with limits and boundaries, your lack of flexibility is a turn off to clients and customers.

This couldn't be further from the truth.

This practice of putting together a strategic schedule actually opens you up to abundance AND imprints into the universe that you are ready to receive your ideal clients that fit into your premier slots.

How does that feel? Yeah…I'm guessing a little funky.

Here is why - we were taught to use a calendar backwards. We are always scheduling things in it for other people. Did you ever notice how you are hardly ever a priority on your own calendar? You will switch something personal to fit in a client…you will shift and ask if you can arrive late for a lunch or dinner date to get that last client in. You are constantly breaking dates with yourself.

Let me ask you a question…

Would you cancel a client appointment because a "better" client came along and wanted the slot? NO! So why do you reschedule yourself constantly in your own calendar?

Who is your best client?

It's you, my friend.

If you don't treat yourself nice, or make yourself a priority, neither will your clients. You will attract people who abuse your time, switch appointments last minute or just not show up at all. Think long and hard about that. Have you already experienced this?

So here's the deal...start getting used to the fact that YOU are your best client. Start creating non-negotiables in your calendar. Because if you're not going to prioritize yourself, who will?

Here the beauty of this little nugget. Once you create this ideal schedule – on your terms – it's automatically imprinted into the universe.

Kick back and watch what starts to happen.

Miraculously, your ideal clients fit oh so well into your new schedule. Gone are the days of chaos...and crappy clients! Now that's synergy and balance, baby. Time for you, time for them. How happy is this marriage going to be?

When working on your schedule, here are a few suggestions to help you create this.

Step #1 – Choose your non-negotiables. This is where your life gets scheduled first. These are your workouts, meal times, or even walks in the park. Once you have take care of you, make time for the triplets in your life: family, friends and fun. These are date nights, girl's night out, birthday celebrations, vacations, and phone calls to mom. Put these in first before any thought of client times.

Step #2 – Pick three days to see clients. Think about if you like to work over consecutive days or if you like a break in between. For example, see clients Tuesday through Thursday, and block out times accordingly. Be sure to leave 15 minutes in between sessions to give you a chance to go to the bathroom or get a drink of water. You are laughing now, but do you know how many people don't pee during the day? Sheesh!

Step #3 – Choose one day for administrative tasks. Yes…the full day. You will need it! These are filing, getting together papers, making client notes, etc. Many people choose Fridays so they can wrap up the week with a clean slate going into the weekend. Ah…that feels oh so good just thinking about it!

Step #4 – Your last open day – make it your marketing day. Use this day to schedule your sales calls and strategy sessions. Build referral partner relationships, or call someone to see if you can book the next speaking gig or sponsorship. Write your newsletter or email sequence. This day is for any activity that can result in money coming through the door.

Now…we're not striving for perfect here. You may have to tweak some things along the way…but at least you get this started. Your commitment will be tested. I assure you! It's exercising a new muscle and just stay with it…you can do this!

Chapter 13
Getting It Together

Let's have a little fun here. You probably know other business owners who fall into these following categories when it comes to their challenges with time management! Here is where you can have a blast and a bit of a chuckle. Take out a pencil and write in someone's name you know that matches these descriptions.

When it comes to managing time, here are the challenges for each entrepreneurial type:

The INTUITIVE will blow up the clock. They are so focused on their work; they will burn through their time and run late for everything. The key to reining in their time is to clock watch... or set a timer so they are not late to every appointment. Who does this remind you of? _____

The HEART CENTERED entrepreneur will give too much in their sales conversations. They will try and solve all the problems and then won't leave a reason for people to work with them. They need to get used to solving one problem – which is painful – they feel like they are not giving enough.

Then, the rest of the problems are what you can focus on in your work together in your program. Who does this sound like? _____

The CARETAKER will cancel dates with themselves. They are wired to keep giving. They will see time they block out for themselves as negotiable, and run the risk of exhausting themselves without rest or replenishment. Who would fit this description? _____

The INNOVATOR will probably have the easiest time sticking to a schedule. But they run the risk of being late for appointments they schedule too early. They don't tend to sleep a lot. They may want to start their day a bit later than most. Who would this be? _____

The last part of the exercise is, where do you see yourself? Which person can YOU relate to?

_____

Now that you have created your schedule, this is where the rubber meets the road. This is what all of that clarity around your time will get you…making money! YES…finally! Now you're ready for it to start flowing in, because you've opened up your "receiving channels." That's what you were doing with your calendar! We'll dive deeper into that concept in another chapter.

For now, you can actually measure how much revenue you can generate based on your time. And if you need to make some tweaks, those adjustments will make more sense to you.

Now that you have blocked out three days a week for clients, you now know how many slots you have available to service those clients. This could come in the form of one on one work, group programs or intensive times.

Let's use an example of someone who has a one-to-one business model for ease.

Here's an example:

My client, Trudy, who is a therapist, has

6 slots open each day
3 days of the week
That means she has a total of 18 client times available each week.

On average, there are 4 weeks in a month. Trudy takes 1 week off from seeing clients each month.

18 slots weekly x 3 weeks she sees clients = 54 open slots Trudy has in a month.

Trudy sees her clients 3 times a month
Each client uses 3 slots
54 divided by 3 = 18

Trudy has room each month for 18 clients at all times.

Take Trudy's example and fill this in for yourself:

# of clients slots open each week:___
# of monthly slots (daily slots x 3 or 4 weeks):___
Monthly slots divided by number of times a client sees you every month:___

Great! Next, this is where we show you the money.

But first, when you have a service-based business, you don't want to be seen as a commodity. You want to get out of the cycle of trading time for money. Why? Because your clients will become clock-watchers and then become distracted. That will diminish their experience with you because they are counting dollars as the clock ticks. If you package your services, you will be able to use the package to fill what it is they want to accomplish. The investment is clear, as well as the benefits and features of what they are going to receive. This is where you have to drive the bus and tell them what they need to be doing in order to get what they want. Create packages based on your experiences with prior clients. You're already up-leveling their experience and creating value without having to justify your hourly fee – because it doesn't exist!

Continuing with Trudy's example, here is how we calculated her monthly income:

18 clients x $500.00 per month = $9,000.00 monthly income

Not too shabby!

But she needs 18 clients at all times to achieve that number. She has to maintain her prospect pipeline. If you don't have a marketing funnel to generate connections, then you can't have sales conversations to turn people into clients. It all works together.

I've created a visual document so you can see how this can work for you. Visit 6figureschedule.com/resource for more detail.

Let your numbers guide you each month to help tell the story of what's happening in your business, and where you need to make tweaks.

If the machine doesn't seem to be humming on all cylinders, here are a few things to check under the hood:

Troubleshooting tip #1: If you're not able to fill your practice, and your client numbers keep hovering around half of your goal number, then you have to step up your marketing efforts. Add more marketing activities to your funnel, which are captured on your marketing calendar.

Troubleshooting tip #2: If you are chock full of marketing activities but aren't getting enough sales conversations, then look at where you are spending your time. Profile the crowd you are hanging around and re-evaluate your target market. You may need dive deeper into finding where your people are hanging out.

Troubleshooting tip #3: If you have filled your client openings, but you aren't hitting your monthly income goal, then you need to look at what you are charging for your packages and programs. Time to raise your prices!

Troubleshooting tip #4: If you're getting a ton of sales conversations, but they aren't turning into clients, then re-evaluate your conversations and how you can use more of your natural working style to shift those conversations.

Here's another thing about money…

Start observing the people you surround yourself with. Does money come easily or are they living month to month? Here's the deal…it's one of those laws of compensation. We tend to earn within 20% of the people we hang out with.

Take that in for a moment…it's powerful stuff.

Does this mean you need to ditch your childhood friend that may be temporarily down on their luck? No. But you can do something else that is extremely powerful.

You see, being a business owner is a solitary proposition by design. It's isolating. Working on your own, with no one else to talk to, and when you're looking for input on ideas, you're it! In order to raise the vibration of your money receiving channels (upcoming chapter), start by aligning yourself with other business owners looking to up-level themselves as well.

This is what is called the "mastermind" concept. Everyone gets what you are up to; and you're all in the same boat trying to achieve many of the same goals for your businesses.

And remember that statistic of earning within 20% of the people you hang out with? Get into a mastermind with other serious business owners who have money goals on par with yours. Hold each other accountable, create a sounding board, and keep each other on track.

Building that momentum raises the vibration that actually carries everyone up together. It's an amazing thing that happens. How cool is that? And the truth be told, no one ever succeeds alone.

We are wired for connection. Everyone has help. The biggest names out there have help. Have you ever heard of a board of directors? That's help! And you can achieve that too. You can't do it alone, so why not do it alongside other really cool, fun people looking to change the world with their earning power!?

Chapter 14
Money Bus

You're in good shape here! You have a plan, and you know how to work the plan. And the money should start coming your way! Logically, that means the money would start flowing in like water, right? Well, we have one more area to tackle when it comes to money.

And it all has to do with a story.

It's your money story. Money stories are like belly buttons, everybody has one!

Let me explain what I mean by introducing you to your new bus…the money bus. It's a big green bus, and it can carry lots and lots of money!

You can have the best-laid plans of how to get money onto the bus. That's what we've done so far in the previous chapters. The thing is, your plan isn't what's driving the bus. The plan is merely a passenger in the front seat with the directions of where to go to get the money. It's sort of like the GPS or the navigator. You need the plan, but more importantly….

You need the driver.

So who IS driving this bus anyway?

It's your money story. She's driving your potential for wealth. She's got the keys and is running this show. It's time to get acquainted with this chick, because she's dragging your money bus all around town.

There are plenty of potential piles of cash at each bus stop, and the plan navigates you to it, but how much you receive depends on your driver. Your bus can pull up at any stop, but it doesn't mean she - your money story - is opening up the doors!

You get me? Let me clarify.

Knowing your money story is your key to understanding why you could be doing everything "right" in your efforts to build your business, and still not cashing in.

You've got a plan, that GPS or the passenger with the map, and it can steer you right to the money, but if you don't let the money on the bus, or you stuff the bus with huge piles of money and bury yourself, or you if let the money fly out the window, you are not living your wealth potential.

Identifying how your money story drives the bus is essential to having your six-figure dream.

Let's look at your entrepreneurial type and see what money story may be driving your bus:

The INTUITIVES often struggle with not facing situations head on when it comes to money. Money can be scary, and can even be a mystery. Maybe you never knew where money came from when you were a kid.

If you're a classic money avoider, this is where we need you to slowly take your head out of the sand. You will need a plan to start consistently looking at money, your bank statements (yes, you have to open them!) and your income and your expenses.

Your lesson here is to be more mindful of money and really understand the energy behind how it comes to you, and how it leaves you.

Picture this; you see a pile of money on the side of the road. Noticing this can actually paralyze an intuitive type. Money can sometimes make Intuitives a bit nervous. Why? Because, money is energy! Money represents more energy to process and manage. So sometimes, Intuitives will look at money like it is too much work to handle. So opening up the doors to bring that money onto their bus, they see it as a challenge. There's just too much work and responsibility around having all of that ching laying around. And in turn, you Intuitives may shut down and not want to deal. You think that you're better off keeping that bus moving, breezing past the money! Can you see how silly that is? But yet, that's what you're doing. Accountability and responsibility when it comes to money is the muscle to strengthen here.

HEART CENTERED entrepreneurs often walk around with their business breakeven number in their heads. You will know at all times what you need to bring in to cover all of the expenses. Your thoughts of "just enough" money and "the rest is gravy" will keep you at the same level month after month.

Your struggle lies with moving your money dial. Meaning, being able to finally break through your income level that has stayed the same for a long time because you're thinking about making "enough." When you realize this, then you will take action. But it won't happen overnight. Your bus driver is hauling ass throughout town with a specific dollar figure in her head. As soon as she's picked up just enough to meet that dollar figure, she calls it quits for the day. Challenge those "just enough" thoughts. Think about all the lives and hearts you can touch with an abundance of money!

Now the CARETAKER is a fun soul! You are the ones always buying the round of drinks at the bar, or showering people with gifts on birthdays. You tend to not be mindful of your spending. If you think buying something for someone else will make them happy, you are all over it. You Caretakers will reach into your pocket so quickly to help someone else out that you won't even think to keep something for yourself so that you can eat that day! Caretakers have very narrow receiving channels. You are so used to spending money, you may not have ever learned how to receive money. So money will go out faster than it comes in. It will also show up in fits and starts.

Essentially, your bus driver is picking up money, along with loads of unexpected expenses. And then she's taking off with the door, windows and emergency exits wide open while watching the money fly out the window! Caretakers often feel like they can't get ahead because they always have unexpected expenses coming up. They get done cleaning up one disaster, and then another one strikes. Once you realize you need to learn how to receive, the money will start to stick around for longer and will eventually shut down those lofty unexpected expenses.

The INNOVATORS are a thrifty bunch. If people hang around you for long enough, they might hear the squeaks of your wallet! You love a good bargain. And if you can do something for yourself rather than pay for it, you think that makes you happy, but really, it winds up annoying you that you have spent so much time on doing it yourself in the end. But you'd rather save the money than pay someone else.

You're a big saver. You may have heard talk as a kid to "save for a rainy day." It's just that no one taught you what a rainy day looked like! In essence, you have a high level of commitment to safety and security, and in turn, don't even realize you are living a life of deprivation.

The driver of your bus is picking up all of the money and holding it hostage on the bus, and even trying to stuff more money on the bus because it's waiting for a rainy day. It's a constant fight with money. With this money story, you're not letting your driver have bathroom breaks, nor a lunch break, and you're certainly not springing for medical coverage. You're holding her hostage until she collects all the money! But your safety number keeps moving up and up and up. So the Innovator's lesson is to open yourself to abundance and get help using experts (and paying for them!) so you can see your vision come to fruition.

Chapter 15
Construction Ahead

Can you see how understanding who is driving your money bus matters?

You've got all the nuts and bolts strategy now. You've got the steps to create that Six- Figure Schedule. You have it all! Seriously, you do! And now you can see how to address your money story to drive that bus straight to Boom Town.

You also need to understand that you will hit some construction bumps along the roadways. And to tell you the truth, they aren't so mysterious. These land mines usually pop up in consistent areas. Know that what you will go through along your journey is completely normal…and this too shall pass.

The roadblocks have to do with mindset. Successful entrepreneurs have mastered these areas, but you will rarely ever hear them talk about this. These are the dragons they have slayed. This is where fear, worry and anxiety all intersect.

All successful entrepreneurs step into the unknown on a daily basis. And some days it feels like you're just side stepping the land mines. Knowing what you are up against can help you navigate the terrain better.

Think of it as slaying dragons on your way to riches. Don't bother looking for them, they will find you! It's all in how you handle them that will get you to the other side. It's all revealed in your eyes. And that's why I love iridology. It really helps a person identify their type and navigate to their "true North."

Be ready for these roadblocks:

The Big "P":   So here's the deal, many of you are suffering from the big "P." Perfection. Some people never get past this roadblock. I hear people say, "My website needs to be perfect before I start finding clients." "I can't write a newsletter unless I know exactly what to say." "Oh, I'm not ready to do this!"

I've also found that those of you who think you're procrastinators, it's actually not true. It's just a bad case of perfection.

Perfection keeps us stuck. Soon, it turns into overwhelm. And if you're trying to generate revenue, this means no dinero to your bottom line. Releasing from this cycle of perfection keeps you moving forward. So how do you do that?

Well, I have a really powerful tip: Replace "perfection" in your vocabulary with the word "done."

Trying to find the "right" networking event? Pick one and done. Have a website that needs copy? Just get it done. Got a newsletter due to go out? Get it done!

Let's see the power of "done" in action. I recently had a tight deadline for a sponsorship. With so many things to do, this is how it could have gone down: infinite hours of design for the perfect promotional banner, unlimited review of perfectly paired colors, and rewrite after rewrite of copy. Our team could have futzed all day and all night over all of it! Instead, my assistant and I set a timer, worked in thirty-minute time blocks over a one-week period. It created focus and commitment to getting things done.

Nothing is ever perfect, but a lot of new clients show up when you get things done!

Hiding: In one way or another, we are all hiding in our businesses. Many hide without knowing it, or have a deeper darker reason. Whatever the reason, when you get to the root of this, the roadblock lays not just with the fear of being seen, or simply stepping to the front of the room; but the underlying fear is of judgment.

For some, this can show up as a result of growing up in the midst of trauma. Perhaps with a parent who struggled with issues around an addiction or possible wartime experiences, or where there was shame around the family situation. This is a common trait ingrained at a very young age. Being in the middle of this unwanted situation, caused you to hide and it continues to keep you there. You strived to make yourself invisible as a survival technique. In addition, you just didn't want to have to deal with outsiders, trying to explain your situation. It was just too exhausting, and you weren't up for the judgments that went along with it.

Add being a woman to that equation, since you are traditionally the support system behind men who are the hunters and gathers, you were naturally placed behind the scenes, never front and center stage.

So here's the deal, if you want a successful business, you have to be seen.

Period.

Energetically, if you hide, so will the money.

Start stepping to the front of the room. Maybe in the past, your corporate career made you feel like no one heard you, and no one cared what you had to say. I know, I felt the same way at times.

I promise you, all you have to do is find your tribe - the people's lives that you can make a difference in. Therein lies your target market! They will devour and hang on your every word. It's a shift in audience, so get out there and find ways to be seen through speaking, networking, sponsorships, or even writing a book (wink, wink) or a newsletter. Even if you are nervous, you go and do it. It's the simplest and greatest marketing strategy on the planet!

Getting Help: For all you hyper self-reliants out there, asking for help is truly difficult. This roadblock will show up pretty quickly for you.

As women, we have learned early on to be autonomous and to multi-task. Our mothers did it, our grandmothers did it. The thing is, as a business owner, that only gets you a one-way ticket to burn out.

You have to start letting people know what you are up to, and when people offer to help...YOU TAKE IT WITH OPEN ARMS!

Start slowly, maybe enlisting your partner or your mother-in-law to watch the kids one night a week so you can go get some things done. Next, hire some administrative help for a few hours a week so you can focus on revenue generating activities.

You can't do this entrepreneurial journey alone. Between the isolation of being a business owner and the "do it yourself" mentality, this staunch refusal to get support will put you out of business faster than you can say boo.

I promise you, doing everything yourself, working countless hours, and exhausting yourself will not get you business owner of the year award. And it certainly won't get you to the front of the line at the pearly gates either. There's no reward for suffering.

The Voices: You know those voices inside of your head. News flash! That voice only gets louder as you jump deeper into entrepreneurship. It will riddle you with doubts. It may say things like, "Who am I to do this? I can't do this! I can't have this! I am not good enough! What if I fail?" Worse, "What if people see me fail? What if it's not perfect? What if something goes wrong?"

Did I hit on at least one thing your voice says to you? We all have the voice, and it never stops.

Seasoned entrepreneurs have the same voices going on in their heads as they did when they started. But here's the difference, they have learned to quiet the voices.

They learn to use the voices to their advantage. When the negative self-talk comes up, it's just their indicator system telling them they are entering unknown territory, and they are about to learn something new. That's it! The voices don't ever stop; you just learn how to handle them differently.

First, start by identifying the underlying fear. Let's use the example of something I hear often, "I can't do this" or "I can't have this." Ask yourself, where in your life did someone tell you that you could not do or have something? Was it back in school when you tried out for a sports team and you weren't picked? Was it a parent telling you can't cross the street by yourself?

Here's the secret: This belief of not being able to have what you want is in the form of a contract. This is a contract you signed a long time ago with yourself. Your childhood self signed a contract and committed to "Not being able to do this." Think about it for a moment.

Let's fast-forward to your 30-40-50-something-year-old self. Here's where the magic happens.

It's contract re-negotiation time.

Here is where you have the power to put in place a new contract that resides in your belief system. So the new contract may read, "I can do anything I want to, as long as I commit to it. And I can help more people if I can do it, and show others how too."

Congratulations, you've got a new contract baby!

Here is how the voice showed up for my client Elaine:

Elaine has a voice that kept coming up saying she can't be wrong. Ever. She put pressure on herself to always do and be right. There was nothing right about being wrong. If she did things wrong, she didn't get praise. She didn't get attention. Which in turn meant she did not get love.

In this case, Elaine's voice was trying to tell her something.

Her voice needed just the opposite of what it believed to quiet down. It needed to know that being wrong was right. And what was right about it? In not having to perfect, she could explore. The freedom to be "wrong" would teach her how to talk to her ideal clients, what type of clients she truly loved to serve, and how to constantly keep improving her services. Being wrong implies there is only one right. It implies there is no choice and only one way to do things. Her voice needed freedom.

We all have our voices and we all learn to handle them. You will too.

So when you see a seasoned professional take a stage to talk to umpteen numbers of people, they are just as nervous as all get out as if it was their first time. Their voices are going ba-na-nas. But here is what they do: they have learned how to quiet their internal voices. They recognize its energy, and learning how to harness and handle it that makes it different over time. Harnessing energy begins with not trying to suppress it or be in resistance to it. It's all about allowing it; and using it to propel your excitement on stage, or in any conversation, and to engage with your audience in the form of enthusiasm and charisma.

We are never "perfect" and we never know it all and we never will get it all right.

And that is just fine.

Chapter 16
The E-Shift

I worked on a trading floor for a Wall Street firm and I had a pretty successful career. I thought I was smart, and I had a solid education under my belt. And while I knew starting my own business wouldn't be "easy," I fully expected that I should be successful at it. I had been part of small businesses and start-ups before.

In the beginning, it felt easy. I got a handful of clients early on. I had one offering, and it was covering the expenses. But once those clients completed their time with me, I got to a point where the money wasn't coming in. Then I walked around my office, muttering to myself, "Now what?" I didn't have a clue what to do next. I wondered, "What happened? Why is this so hard? I was able to navigate much more easily in my corporate gig. Why is that?"

That's where the light bulb went off.

Here's what I've discovered.

We were programmed in our corporate careers to act and behave in certain ways. We were rewarded for this, and we became successful with this mentality.

But this mentality doesn't work as an entrepreneur.

For example, we waited for permission and approval for the next steps in our jobs.

I remember needing approval for just about everything, from which hotel I could book when I was traveling, to the people I could bring along with me to see a client. Projects rarely moved forward without getting that "committee approval." Does any of this sound familiar?

I got stuck in my business because I was seeking permission for the next "right" thing to do. Because we got pay raises in our corporate job by doing the right thing. But as an entrepreneur, there is no committee, no approval, no sure next right thing. You learn that doing something is better than nothing, and we just have to keep trying different things to see what works, instead of waiting to be told what the next right thing to do is. WE are the permission grantors.

I also believed I had to have everything figured out and perfect before I could actually "do it" or "share it." When you work in a corporate environment, this is what's expected and rewarded.

But here's the real deal... when you're an entrepreneur, that will only keep you stuck doing things that aren't going to make you money and result in frustration and exhaustion. And you will be on the never-ending search for approval.

We've been taught a certain way to be successful. It worked really well as an employee, but it doesn't translate into success as a business owner.

Completely counter-intuitive!

So many women entrepreneurs tell me, "Debra, I don't understand why my business isn't working. I'm feeling stuck, and I just need to get this right."

If you can relate, ask yourself....

Where does this show up for you in your business?
Whose approval do you think you need to get?
Where are you trying to get everything perfect before rolling anything out the door?
Where are you getting stuck as a result of waiting for permission?
Was there a project that never seemed to get off the ground?
Were there countless meetings over every step of progress with projects and countless people you had to inform?
Was there someone there that just wouldn't make a decision because they didn't want responsibility if the project failed?

Welcome to the E-shift – the transition from employee to entrepreneur.

See where this may be showing up in your business today. Find a trusted and supportive colleague or mentor who gets what you're up to. Have them serve as the guide or temporary permission grantor. Eventually, you'll increase your confidence in making your own decisions.

Here's the pay off in hiring a mentor:

If you stay on this path of looking for approval, staying stuck or find yourself procrastinating because you're caught up in perfection, you're on a path for blame. Blaming yourself for not figuring this out. The truth is, no one figures it out alone. And you can avoid the next cycle after all of this self-blame – it's the cycle of quitting. Then you give up.

So if you're wondering, why you were so successful in corporate, but being a business owner is pissing you off, look no further! Step into the E-shift!

Chapter 17
Receiving Channels

When is comes to our energy, time and money, there is one important area to focus on that no one seems to notice.

It's called your receiving channels. I've mentioned receiving channels earlier and now we can delve a bit more into what I am talking about.

Do you know how wide or narrow your receiving channels are?

Well, if you're not making the money you want and deserve, take note of this chapter. Get your highlighter out and a pencil. Dog ear the pages if have to…because here is what's happening for you…

As women, we were programmed at a very young age to help out, lend a hand, and give. "It's better to give than receive" is a message you heard quiet often. And in chronic fashion.

But it's actually not true. It's another universal law around energy that history seemed to keep all to itself, not to be shared. And of course, I love you, and I wouldn't dare keep this to myself! Here goes…

You can only give in equal proportion to what you receive.

Someone is screaming horse pucky right now (and it's probably you, Caretaker!) Just hold the phone for a minute.

You can only give so much, and then you start to break down. If you do not open yourself up to receive, or replenish, you get into a state of exhaustion.

We also think, the more we give, the more we are helping people. It's actually the other way around.

If we give without replenishment, then we aren't able to give our best selves. We've just stretched ourselves too thin! So how does that translate into how we serve our clients?

I had a massage therapist in New York City I used to go to. She was fantastic! Petite in stature, but hands like a three hundred pound man. Boy, could she wrestle those knots!

But here was her deal…

She was constantly over worked. She would say yes to everyone that called for an appointment, and constantly squeezed clients into her schedule. That made her run behind on most of her appointments.

At the end of my workday, I would see her at night. By then, she was so tired; and over extended. I never got the massage I really needed from her. She was good when she was rested! As soon as she would start the massage, I knew what kind of day she had. And I was paying the price for her over commitments.

You see how the constant giving can backfire?

That massage therapist lost a client in me. And I was willing to pay for her expertise. But she wasn't showing up in the way I knew she could, and in the way I needed her to.

Over-giving shows up in your time, your energy…and in turn, in your money. It's all connected!

So if you're not making the money you want AND deserve, check out the status of your receiving channels.

In iridology, I can see how narrow women's receiving channels are.

Start exercising the opening of those receiving channels. You're fine in the giving department – that's not the issue!

If someone offers you help, take it. And without the chronic feeling that you have to give right back.

If you work a long day, be sure to build in rest for the next day.

Build in vacations to your schedule.

Make requests of the people around you to help you around the house.

The key is BALANCE when it comes to giving and receiving. If you over-give, then you're too tired to receive. Capice?

That's the name of the giving game. Now, go do it! Then watch how your entire life shifts for you. The exhaustion fades away, the chronic quid pro quo becomes a non-issue, and the money starts coming in like gangbusters. Oh, and you get time off and an actual vacation out of the deal too. Not too shabby for a small shift in mindset!

Chapter 18
Stai zitta!

When we work hard, we feel like we are humming along. We feel like staying in action is the name of the game. Don't stop, we are on a roll!

But sometimes we come up against challenges that we just can't solve. Then we turn to working harder, longer to solve the problem.

Ah…the habits from corporate come creeping in again! Work until you solve the problem!

Here's what tends to work best: Walk away from the table, ma'am.

Stai zitta we say in Italian. In English, it means, "to shut up" or "just stop."

Push your chair away from your desk, and leave the problem on the table. Shut the door behind you. Don't worry; it's not going anywhere!

So now you will ask, how the heck am I going to solve the problem if I just walk away?

Leave it to your partner!

"Huh? But I don't have a partner in my business!"

Here's the deal….I encourage you to take a partner in your business.

And I'm not talkin' some guru or angel investor.

The partner in your business – is the universe.

It's the universal energy that is always working in your favor and on your behalf. Always striving to put you on the right track, it's guiding you where you need to go.

Newsflash – you can't control the universe.

Oh and it has a gift for you! Here is it…. your pink slip. It just told you "you're fired!" The universe has just fired you from trying to control everything in your business.

The universe is always going to work on your behalf, whether you try to steer it or not.

For all of you left-brained, this-needs-to-make-sense-show-me-the-proof people out there, I can't. It's not a tangible concept.

All I can tell you is…I'm a left brained "gotta make it happen or else it doesn't happen" kind of gal. I tried this mumbo jumbo, and the darn thing worked. Plain and simple, it just works!

I call it the silver platter treatment. Imagine asking for what you want…then actually getting it without having to lift a finger!

Ah-ma-zing.

Here's how it works…

When you have a problem that is taking so much time and energy, you're in the mode of depletion and exhaustion. The laws of the universe say that all you need to do is – stop.

Be still, walk away. It has the answers you are looking for. But if you're too wrapped up in your head searching for the answer, you've closed yourself off to having the answer come in.

Essentially, you're dancing tango with the problem, and not letting a new partner cut in on the dance. There could be a better dance partner, but you're not willing to give up with this one because it's familiar!

When you stop and walk away, you've just opened up your receiving channels.

You need down time to open up those receiving channels.

Have you ever gotten up in the morning, taken a shower, been brushing your teeth, looking into the mirror, then all of a sudden an idea pops in? And it happens to be the solution to the problem that you have been wracking your brain over?

It came that easily…and then you're pissed. You spent so much time on that problem and here it is? Popping up in the middle of your morning routine!?

You've had this happen before…I know you have. Just walking the dog, going for a yoga class. Once you take the brainpower off of the problem, voila…the answer shows up.

That's your business partner, the universe, working on your behalf.

And this is precisely why you need to build time off and vacation in your schedule intentionally. Being away from your business turns it over to your partner and pays you dividends beyond what you could have done staying back in the office and busting your buns.

Here is an example:

I did two roadshows back to back one month. I knew I would need replenishment after this, so I scheduled a week off at the end of month. One week of work and follow up calls, and then I was off.

Here was my problem, I had so many great opportunities to follow up with, but I knew I was exhausted. I was impatient, worried and nervous letting the rest of my sales calls wait until after I got back. I was concerned that I would miss out on getting new clients.

Well, I had a great sales week before my vacation. I signed on every person I spoke with to work with me. Now my anxiety and nervousness was through the roof! I'm breaking the momentum…how could I do this?

Well, I trusted in my business partner, and took the vacation with my family. Which was totally awesome…my daughter skied for the first time and I filmed every minute of it!

I had my week off, and then came back to more sales calls the following week. Guess what happened? I closed even more business that week, and in record time. I had my best month ever in my business, generating multiple 5 figures of business...in only 4 hours...with a week long vacation in between.

That's a testament to opening up your receiving channels, problem solving, and letting your partner run your business while you are away.

I hope your next step is booking your long awaited vacation to Maui before you turn the pages of this chapter!

Chapter 19
True Impact

Do you know the definition of wealth?

I believe strategic advisor and business consultant, Dan Kennedy, says it best. I'm going to switch up the gender references...but here goes,

"The individual who gets to use her time in ways that bring her great joy and fulfillment, who gets to do work that is genuinely personally interesting, who gets to choose her associates, and who gets to make some kind of a contribution to fellow mankind, wakes up wealthy every morning and goes to bed wealthy every night, regardless of her bank balance."

Listen, I want you to make the money...no doubt about that! But once the money starts flowing in, and your money story comes into balance, this is ultimately what true wealth is.

Herein lies the power, combining this definition with your WHY. You become unstoppable and outrageously happy all at the same time. Life is good!

The thing is, this book isn't just about how you can make a ton of money and still have time enough to enjoy it. It's actually much bigger than that.

You see, if we all commit to working in a balanced manner, open ourselves up to receive money, get clear on what we want, working with our strengths and hiring others to help with our weaknesses, we can change a generation. Yep. THE BIG SHIFT – starts with you. If you commit to shifting to a life where you don't have to invest in struggle, what a better place the world would be.

No more over working. No more fears around money. People would have time to spend with their families and they in turn would feel heard and understood. Kids will feel loved and supported – and feel like they matter. Everyone would be happier and daily complaints would all but disappear.

Our bodies would function on a superior level since it would no longer have to bear all of the nervous system stress. There would be no room for fear and worry. People would be healthier, heart attacks would decrease, and endocrine system cancers would all but disappear. We'd be happy, healthy and able to enjoy a life for as long as we'd like to live!

You have a lot to give, and we need what you have.

And what you do can create possibilities for others.

The next generation needs to see you get this…without the struggle…so we contribute on a higher level, and receive everything that is waiting for us.

It's available for the taking. And it's available to every single one of us. You can't even imagine what is awaiting you!

But isn't it just fun exploring it?

Now go and get it!

Struggle is Optional...

Get Debra's best advice how to make a big shift fast. In an exclusive chapter that wasn't sent to print, learn the one thing that's keeping most people stuck down the rabbit hole when it comes to their business, and the daily practice you can do everyday to keep the revenue rolling in. Download this chapter if you are willing to take a leap. It's powerful, it's jaw dropping, and it works.

To download this chapter now, visit 6figureschedule.com/secretchapter

Debra Angilletta is a business strategist + behavioral iridologist who helps budding entrepreneurs ditch the anxiety (and countless draining hours often associated with it) so that they can build six-figure businesses. Tired of the corporate treadmill, she left a 20-year Wall Street career with clear and non-negotiable priorities; to create a thriving business AND have time to enjoy her young daughter and family. With only 20 hours a week to devote to work, Debra mastered the keys to creating a successful business on her terms. Now she teaches you how to streamline your schedule and package your business for profit so that you can enjoy it all and have the business and life of your dreams.